STEM *trailblazer* BIOS

PROGRAMMING PIONEER
ADA LOVELACE

VALERIE BODDEN

Lerner Publications ◆ Minneapolis

Lerner Publications Company
A division of Lerner Publishing Group, Inc.
241 First Avenue North
Minneapolis, MN 55401 U.S.A.

For reading levels and more information, look up this title at www.lernerbooks.com.

Content Consultant: Valeria Aurora, cofounder of the Ada Initiative

Library of Congress Cataloging-in-Publication Data

Names: Bodden, Valerie.
Title: Programming pioneer Ada Lovelace / by Valerie Bodden.
Description: Minneapolis : Lerner Publications, 2017. | Includes bibliographical references and index.
Identifiers: LCCN 2015049786 (print) | LCCN 2016000530 (ebook) | ISBN 9781512407846
   (library bound : alkaline paper) | ISBN 9781512413038 (paperback : alkaline paper) | ISBN
   9781512410877 (eb pdf)
Subjects: LCSH: Lovelace, Ada King, Countess of, 1815–1852—Juvenile literature. | Women
   mathematicians—Great Britain—Biography—Juvenile literature. | Women computer
   programmers—Great Britain—Biography—Juvenile literature. | Mathematicians—Great Britain—
   Biography—Juvenile literature. | Computer programmers—Great Britain—Biography—Juvenile
   literature. | Computers—Great Britain—History—19th century—Juvenile literature. | Computer
   algorithms—History—19th century—Juvenile literature.
Classification: LCC QA29.L72 B63 2017 (print) | LCC QA29.L72 (ebook) | DDC 510.92--dc23

LC record available at http://lccn.loc.gov/2015049786

Manufactured in the United States of America
1 – PC – 7/15/16

The images in this book are used with the permission of: Public Domain, pp. 4, 10, 21; © David Edwin/Library of Congress, p. 5; © Photos.com/Thinkstock, pp. 6, 25; © Chronicle/Alamy Stock Photo, p. 7; Detroit Publishing Company/Library of Congress, p. 8; Library of Congress, p. 11; © Everett Collection Inc/Alamy Stock Photo, p. 13; © Pictorial Press Ltd/Alamy Stock Photo, pp. 14, 24; © Ann Ronan Pictures/Heritage Images/Glow Images, p. 16; © Andrew N. Gagg/Alamy Stock Photo, p. 18; © Science Source, p. 19; © Photos 12/Alamy Stock Photo, p. 23; © famouspeople/ Alamy Stock Photo, p. 27; © Paul Clarke CC2.0, p. 28.

Front Cover: © Pictorial Press Ltd/Alamy Stock Photo.

CONTENTS

Chapter 1

Ada began studying math and science as early as four years old.

LORD BYRON'S DAUGHTER

Ada Byron was born on December 10, 1815, in London, England. Her father was the famous poet Lord Byron. When Ada was only one month old, her father left her mother. Ada never saw him again.

Ada's mother, Annabella, did not want Ada to grow up to be like her father. So she decided to rein in Ada's imagination by making sure she studied practical subjects such as mathematics.

Rumors spread about Lord Byron's irresponsible behavior as he traveled the world.

Most women in the 1800s did not receive a strong education.

At that time, there were few schools for girls in England. Most girls received little education. Many people even thought that women's brains were weaker than men's. Girls were taught only what they needed to take care of a home and family.

But from age four, Ada studied with tutors that her mother hired. Ada had lessons in math, science, French, and **logic**. Annabella wanted her daughter to be well-educated. But she did not want Ada to have a career in math or science. That was not considered proper for women of the time.

By the time she was eight years old, Ada had fallen in love with math. She also read articles about new scientific

Ada was dedicated to her studies but also dreamed up new inventions.

Steamboats, similar to this one seen in Detroit, Michigan, in the 1800s, fascinated Ada.

WALK-IN-THE-WATER

WALK-IN-THE-WATER

discoveries with delight. In 1826, when Ada was ten, her mother took her on a tour of Europe. Ada was especially impressed by the steamboats she saw in Switzerland.

After returning home, the young girl continued to think about the possibilities of steam power. When she was twelve, Ada decided to make a flying machine. She planned to power it with a steam engine. She studied a dead bird her cat had brought in to learn more about wings. Then she made herself a pair of wings from paper and wire.

Ada was often sick as a child. When she was thirteen, she became seriously ill. Doctors today think she may have had **measles** or **polio**. The illness **paralyzed** her legs. She had to remain in bed for three years. Ada used the time to continue her studies.

TECH TALK

"I have got a scheme . . . It is to make a thing in the form of a horse with a steam engine on the inside . . . to move an immense pair of wings, fixed on the outside of the horse, in such a manner as to carry it up into the air while a person sits on its back."

—*Ada Byron, age twelve, in a letter to her mother*

Chapter 2

At age seventeen, Ada met the man who would spark her interest in programming.

THINKING LIKE A MAN

By the time she was sixteen, Ada had recovered from her illness and could walk again. The next year, her mother began taking her to gatherings of some of the greatest scholars of the day. These gatherings were often

Charles Babbage is often referred to as the "father of computing."

held at the home of Charles Babbage, a forty-one-year-old mathematician, engineer, and inventor. Ada and Babbage quickly struck up a friendship over their shared love of math. Babbage told Ada about his latest project: a machine called the Difference Engine.

Although computers had not yet been invented, people still needed to make complex calculations to help them in many fields. Calculations were needed to help determine a ship's course, for example. Or they could be used to figure out the strengths of building materials. But the people who needed those calculations often did not know how to make them. Instead, people known as "computers" made these calculations with pen and paper. Then they entered the answers into tables, which could be printed and sold to navigators or builders. These human computers spent thousands of hours making the tables. But when the tables were done, they often included many errors. These errors could have serious consequences. Sometimes they caused ships to run aground.

Babbage's Difference Engine was supposed to change all that. It would automatically do the math and generate the tables. The machine was made up of several columns of stacked gears. Each gear was marked with the numbers zero

TECH TALK

"[Mathematics] constitutes the language through which alone we can adequately express the great facts of the natural world."

—Ada Lovelace, on the significance of Babbage's machine

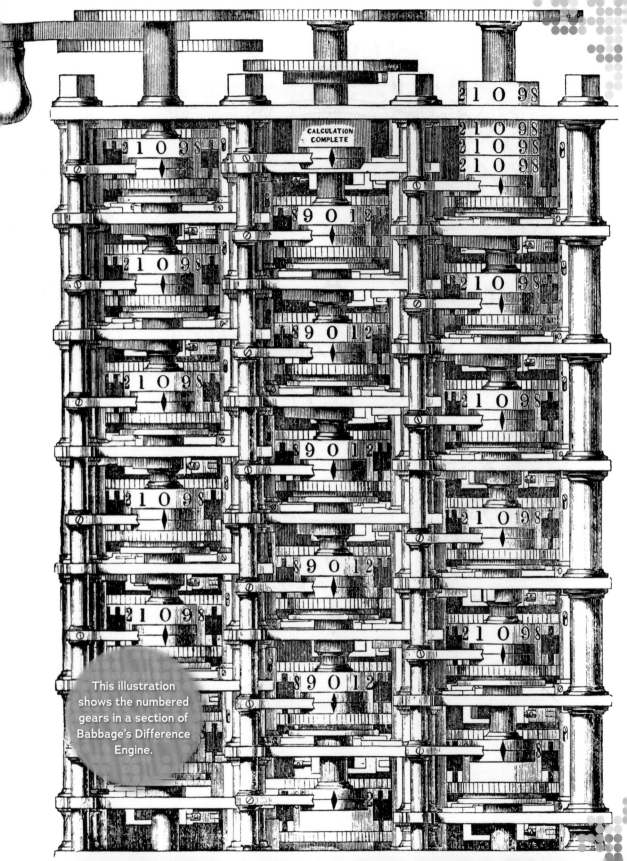

CALCULATION
COMPLETE

This illustration shows the numbered gears in a section of Babbage's Difference Engine.

Even as she took on the duties of a wife and mother, Ada continued to study math.

to nine. When the machine's handle was turned, the numbers on the columns of gears would be added together. Other gears showed the results, which were also stamped onto paper.

Babbage demonstrated a small model of the machine for Ada. She immediately understood its potential to quickly create error-free tables. Babbage received government funding for the Difference Engine. But he never created the full machine, which would have required twenty-five thousand precisely made parts.

After seeing the Difference Engine, Ada pleaded with Babbage to become her tutor. Babbage refused, saying he was too busy. But the two wrote to each other regularly.

Ada also talked with other leading mathematicians. Among them was Mary Somerville, one of the most famous female mathematicians and scientists of the time. Somerville soon became a teacher, friend, and mentor to Ada. She sent Ada math books and problems to solve.

Ada saw math and science in action when her mother took her on a tour through England's factories. There she saw firsthand the effects of the Industrial Revolution, a period of rapid progress in the development of machinery and factories. The Revolution had begun in England in the late 1700s and later spread to other parts of the world.

A man prepares punched cards for a Jacquard loom in 1844.

Ada marveled at how new machinery was changing the way things were made. She especially admired the Jacquard loom. This machine used a series of punch cards—cards with holes punched in specific places—to provide instructions to a weaving loom. These instructions told the loom what pattern to create in the fabric. Different sets of cards could be used to create different patterns.

In 1835, at the age of nineteen, Ada married William King. King later inherited the title Earl of Lovelace. Soon afterward, Ada began calling herself Ada Lovelace. Her official title was Lady Lovelace.

TECH TALK

"The power of thinking on these matters which Lady L. has always shown . . . has been . . . utterly out of the common way for any beginner, man or woman. Had any young beginner . . . shown the same power, I should have prophesied . . . that they would have certainly made him an original mathematical investigator, perhaps of first-rate eminence."

—Augustus De Morgan, on Lovelace's abilities

In 1840, Ada began studying under Augustus De Morgan, one of the top mathematicians of the era. De Morgan wrote to Ada's mother, praising Ada's understanding of mathematical concepts. But at the same time, he worried that Ada thought too much like a man. She did not simply accept his instructions about how to perform mathematical operations. Instead, she questioned him widely about the very foundations of mathematics. De Morgan worried that such thinking might be too strenuous for a woman and could affect her health. But Ada's mother was unconcerned, and Ada continued her studies.

Chapter 3

Punched cards were used in the Difference Engine, as well as in many machines for years to come.

THE FIRST COMPUTER
PROGRAMMER

By the 1840s, Lovelace had become fascinated with a new idea Babbage had begun to tell anyone who would listen. He called it the Analytical Engine. Babbage planned for this machine to be programmed with punch cards similar to those used for the Jacquard loom. The machine would be able to print out a hard copy of its results. The results would also be imprinted onto plaster tablets that could be used to make printing plates for printing presses. That way, many copies of the results could be printed, with less chance for error. Punch cards could be used to store the machine's results, as well.

Babbage's purpose for the new machine was to perform different types of mathematical operations. But Lovelace saw

Lovelace and Babbage exchanged many letters discussing the potential of the Analytical Engine.

TECH TALK

"We believe that [the Analytical Engine] . . . surpasses its predecessors, both in the extent of the calculations which it can perform . . . and in the absence of all necessity for the intervention of human intelligence during the performance of its calculations."

—Ada Lovelace, Notes by the Translator, *1843*

that it had greater potential. She thought it would be a general-purpose computer that could be used for more than math. She realized the computer could operate on any form of data that could be represented by numbers. It might even be used to create music or images.

Babbage traveled across Europe seeking funding to build the Analytical Engine. In 1842, an Italian mathematician named Luigi Menabrea attended one of Babbage's lectures. Afterward, he wrote a paper about the Analytical Engine. The paper was written in French, so Lovelace translated it into English. But she didn't stop there. She also added more than nineteen thousand words of her own notes, titling them *Notes by the Translator.*

Lovelace described the process of generating Bernoulli numbers in this table in Note G of her *Notes*.

In her notes, Lovelace provided technical information about how the Analytical Engine would work. She said the machine would weave mathematical equations in the same way that the Jacquard loom wove flowers and leaves. Lovelace's final note, known as Note G, is widely considered to be the first computer program. In it, Lovelace laid out an **algorithm**, or step-by-step instructions, for programming the Analytical Engine. She showed how punch cards could be used to make the machine generate Bernoulli numbers, a complex sequence of numbers produced by a specific mathematical formula.

Within her algorithm, Lovelace included what are today known as loops and subroutines. Loops are sections of instructions that repeat until a desired result is reached. A subroutine is a section of code that performs a specific job. The larger program can run that code whenever needed. Lovelace also included the idea of conditional branching. This means the machine would use the results of its calculations to determine what to do next.

In her *Notes*, Lovelace also stressed what the Analytical Engine could not do. It could not think on its own. She emphasized that the machine had to be programmed by a human. But she also saw that the Analytical Engine might someday be used to solve problems that had long been considered impossible. She thought it might even help discover new problems.

Lovelace's translation and notes were published in 1843 in *Scientific Memoirs*, a popular scientific journal of the time.

TECH TALK

"All this was impossible for you to know by intuition and the more I read your notes the more surprised I am at them."

—*Charles Babbage to Ada Lovelace*

Researchers built this model of the Analytical Engine based on Babbage's notes.

Lovelace did not put her name on them because it was considered improper for women to publish scholarly articles. Instead, she used her initials, A. A. L. The paper was positively received. But it did not lead to funding for the Analytical Engine. The machine was never built.

Chapter 4

Lovelace had a wide range of interests in her short life.

LEAVING A LEGACY

After Lovelace's paper was published, she and Babbage remained friends. But they never worked together on another project. Lovelace felt she could not do much more with the Analytical Engine as long as it was not built. So

Although Michael Faraday did not receive much education, he made important discoveries about electricity.

she turned to new interests. One of those interests was **electromagnetism**, then being studied by noted scientist Michael Faraday. Lovelace began to write to Faraday and attend his lectures.

Lovelace also developed an interest in the relationship between electricity and the human mind and body. She wondered whether the body operated similarly to a machine. Her goal was to describe the workings of the brain in mathematical terms.

Lovelace's studies were cut short when she became ill with cancer in 1851. She died the next year, at the age of thirty-six. After her death, Lovelace's achievements were largely forgotten for nearly one hundred years. But in the

1940s, her *Notes by the Translator* were rediscovered. They helped inspire scientists who were working on designs for the first computers. One of those scientists was Alan Turing. Like Lovelace, Turing wanted to develop a general-purpose computer that could be programmed to perform different tasks. Later computer developers also used concepts first described in Lovelace's *Notes*, including loops, subroutines, and conditional branching.

Turing also gave a name to Lovelace's theory that machines would never be able to think. He called it Lady Lovelace's Objection. Turing disagreed with Lovelace. He developed the Turing Test to determine whether a computer could think. To carry out the Turing Test, a person had to ask

Alan Turing's vision for computers was similar to that described in Lovelace's *Notes*.

a series of questions. Both a human and a computer then answered the questions. If the person asking the questions could not tell which answers came from the computer and which from the human, the machine could be said to think.

In the 1970s, the US Department of Defense named a computer language Ada in honor of Lovelace. And in 2009, international Ada Lovelace Day was founded. The day is celebrated each October. It honors women in science, technology, engineering, and mathematics.

Ada Lovelace was one of the first people to grasp the possibilities of the computer. She saw its potential to manipulate almost any form of data, including music. More than 150 years later, her vision—and more—has been realized.

A speaker gives a presentation at the Royal Institution in London, England, as part of Ada Lovelace Day 2014.

TIMELINE

1815

Ada Byron is born in London, England, on December 10.

1827

At the age of twelve, Lovelace begins working on developing a method for human flight, calling her studies Flyology.

1833

Lovelace meets mathematician Charles Babbage and is intrigued by his Difference Engine.

1840

Lovelace begins to study under mathematician Augustus De Morgan.

1843

Lovelace translates an article about Babbage's Analytical Engine. She adds to it her own *Notes*, which include an algorithm to program the machine.

1852

Lovelace dies of uterine cancer on November 27.

1979

The US government names a computer language Ada, in honor of Lovelace.

2009

International Ada Lovelace Day is founded to honor the achievements of women in science, technology, engineering, and mathematics.

SOURCE NOTES

9   James Essinger, *Ada's Algorithm: How Lord Byron's Daughter Ada Lovelace Launched the Digital Age* (Brooklyn, NY: Melville House, 2014), 54.

12   Walter Isaacson, *The Innovators: How a Group of Hackers, Geniuses, and Geeks Created the Digital Revolution* (New York: Simon & Schuster, 2014), 17.

17   Essinger, *Ada's Algorithm*, 135–36.

21   Essinger, *Ada's Algorithm*, 169–70.

23   Rachel Swaby, *Headstrong: 52 Women Who Changed Science—and the World* (New York: Broadway Books, 2015), 185.

25   Harry Henderson, *Modern Mathematicians* (New York: Facts on File, 1996), 12.

GLOSSARY

algorithm
a series of step-by-step instructions

electromagnetism
the study of how magnetic and electrical fields interact

logic
the study of sound reasoning and relationships between ideas

measles
a disease that spreads easily and causes fever and red spots on the body

paralyze
to make someone unable to move

polio
a disease that affects the spinal cord and can cause paralysis

FURTHER
INFORMATION

BOOKS

Hayes, Amy. *Ada Lovelace.* New York: PowerKids, 2016. Find out more about the early years of computers and Ada Lovelace's impact on the industry.

Indovino, Shaina. *Women in Information Technology.* Broomall, PA: Mason Crest, 2014. Meet other women who influenced computer technology throughout history.

Stanley, Diane. *Ada Lovelace, Poet of Science: The First Computer Programmer.* New York: Simon & Schuster, 2016. Learn more about the pioneering computer programmer.

WEBSITES

Brain POP: Ada Lovelace
**https://www.brainpop.com/technology/computerscience/
adalovelace**
Watch a movie, take a quiz, and play games while learning more about Ada Lovelace.

Computer History Museum: The Babbage Engine
http://www.computerhistory.org/babbage
Learn more about Charles Babbage and his invention of the Babbage Engine.

PBS: A History of the Computer
http://www.pbs.org/nerds/timeline
Discover more about the history of the computer with this interactive timeline.

LERNER

SOURCE™

Expand learning beyond the printed book. Download free, complementary educational resources for this book from our website, www.lerneresource.com.

INDEX

ABOUT THE AUTHOR

Valerie Bodden has written more than 200 nonfiction books for children. Her books have received positive reviews from *School Library Journal*, *Booklist*, *Children's Literature*, *ForeWord Magazine*, *Horn Book Guide*, *VOYA*, and *Library Media Connection*. Bodden lives in Wisconsin with her husband and four young children.